The Awful Australian

By

Valerie Desmond

Edition : Culturea (culurea.fr), 34 Hérault
Contact : infos@culturea.fr
Impression : BOD. Norderstedt (Allemagne)
ISBN : 9791041984596
Date de publication : juillet 2023
Mise en page et maquettage : https://reedsy.com/
Cet ouvrage a été composé avec la police Bauer Bodoni

The Awful Australian

CHAPTER I.

AUSTRALIAN POLITICS.

This strange, topsy-turvey country, not content with having fruit with stones on the outside, has made the unique experiment of handing over its government to its peasantry! Other lands have at times fallen under the sway of the hoi-polloi, but this has always been temporary, and the result of some hysterical upheaval. But in Australia this has not been the case. The electors calmly and deliberately voted the Labour Party into power in April, 1910, and, since then, two of the six ridiculous States that this country of four and a-half millions has divided itself into have also calmly and deliberately decided, by majorities, to entrust their national guidance to butchers and bakers and candlestick-makers.

That any body of people should do this—even in a country where every man and woman, irrespective of education, wealth, or social position has a vote—seems unintelligible to the English visitor. It certainly was unintelligible to me at first. It grew more of a mystery when I saw and heard several of the Labour leaders. Then I saw and heard the Liberal leaders, and I no longer wondered.

Of all the products of Australia, the politician is the least worthy and the least competent. Oratory in this land is in the same embryo condition as gem-cutting or the manufacture of scientific instruments. Generally speaking, there is not in the public life of Australia a speaker who reaches to the standard of mediocrity in England or America. And in speaking, so is it much in the other qualifications that make a politician. The present Prime Minister, Mr. Fisher, I heard in Melbourne just before he left for England. Knowing him to have been a miner, I was prepared. It would be unfair to compare Mr. Fisher with one of our cultured statesmen at home. But put him beside another miner—Mr. Keir Hardie—the comparison is ludicrous. I was told to wait until I heard Mr. Deakin, and, as luck would have it, I did get an opportunity of hearing Mr. Deakin at a social function at Toorak. Mr. Deakin was fluent, I'll say that for him, but to regard him as an orator or even an average public speaker is ridiculous to one accustomed to the polished delivery and deep thought of our English politicians.

Among the minor members of the London County Council are many speakers who stand head and shoulders over Mr. Deakin. I also heard Mr. Hughes, Mr. Tudor, and that amusing gentleman Mr. King O'Malley while I was in Melbourne, but I must admit that I was not deeply impressed. The great ones of the Victorian State Parliament I missed, which is possibly as well, if it bears any resemblance to the State Parliament of New South Wales. In this deliberative Assembly I found the standard even lower than in the Federal Parliament. I was unfortunate—or was I fortunate?—in not being able to hear Mr. McGowen. That gentleman was already in England, upholding the honour of New South Wales by hammering a rivet in a girder and walking three miles along a sewer.

But I heard Mr. Holman and I heard Mr. Wade, and I heard Mr. Edden and Mr. Wood and Mr. Fitzpatrick, and several other funny little men whose names I cannot remember. Mr. Holman reminded me of the Polytechnic young man who apes the style of the Oxford Union. Mr. Wade was a lame and halting speaker, whose thoughts moved slowly, and whose diction was execrable. Mr. Edden reminded me of an old gardener we had at home. Mr. Wood was the colonial excelsis. He has the Australian accent strongly developed, he uses slang indiscriminately, and he is bumptious and aggressive. Mr. Fitzpatrick struck me as a mild man naturally trying hard to be like Mr. Wood. The others were colourless. In point of ability, it was ludicrous to think of these men controlling the destinies of a colony—even one of a paltry million and a-half people. I doubt very much if Mr. Holman or Mr. Wade would ever be elected to the London County Council or even one of the surrounding vestries. If they contrived to do so, they would certainly never go back at the ensuing election. Messrs. Holman and Wade in the London County Council would be simply overwhelmed. The inherent bluster of the Australian might prevent them being shamed to silence by the preponderating ability that surrounded them, but it would not be many days before they were forgotten, overlooked, and not even accorded the dignity of an "also spoke" by the press. To think of such politicians being in the Mother of Parliaments is enough to make the legislative angels weep.

CHAPTER II.

THE AUSTRALIAN ACCENT.

One of the strongest prejudices that one has to overcome when one visits Australia is that created by the weird jargon that passes for English in this country. Created is too mild a term to apply to the process. It comes as a positive shock, and I recall with actual pain the morning I awoke as the mailboat lay at Fremantle breakwater, and I heard this horrible patois filter through my porthole to offend my ear for the first time.

Strangely enough, English people who have lived in the colonies for any length of time grow accustomed to the pronunciation of the Australian, and, worst of all, it insinuates itself into their own language, until it is really difficult to find a resident of more than ten years' standing in Australia who does not sing-song like a native.

The Australian accent has frequently been described by travellers, but none have done justice to its abominations. Many unobservant persons, shuddering through three or four months' experience, have left Australia saying that the people of the island continent use the dialect of the East End of London. This is a gross injustice to poor Whitechapel. Neither the coster of to-day, nor the old-time Cockney of the days of Dickens, would be guilty of uttering the uncouth vowel sounds I have heard habitually used by all classes in Australia. For the dialect of this country differs from those of other lands in being as strongly developed among the educated people as among the peasantry. Were its use restricted to the bullock-driver and the larrikin one could make excuses; but this is not so. Judges, scientists, University graduates, and bottle-gatherers use the same universal Australian esperanto. The doctor, who has attained eminence in Australia, and who, in point of merit, is probably quite up to the standard of the average provincial practitioner at Home, will give such words as "light" and "bright" the same exaggerated vowel sound as the cabman and the bootblack. The barrister will not say, "May your Honour please," but "May-ee yer Honour please." The scientist will refer to "Me researches." There is no such word as "my" in the Australian language. "Me husband, me yacht, me motor," one hears everywhere. But the most striking instance of vowel mispronunciation occurs in respect of the diphthong "ow." A cow is invariably a "keeow," brown is "bree-own," town is "teeown."

So exaggerated is the Australian's rendering of this sound that they actually accuse English people of being in error. "Naturally the difference would strike you," once said a leading Australian journalist to me, with a superior smile; "you English people always say rahnd the tahn and talk about milking a brahn cah." I was too used to Australian self-sufficiency by that time to take offence. The people had ceased to offend me and commenced to amuse me.

But it is not so much the vagaries of pronunciation that hurt the ear of the visitor. It is the extraordinary intonation that the Australian imparts to his phrases. There is no such thing as cultured, reposeful conversation in this land; everybody sings his remarks as if he were reciting blank verse after the manner of an imperfect elocutionist. It would be quite possible to take an ordinary Australian conversation and immortalise its cadences and diapasons by means of musical notation. Herein the Australian differs from the American. The accent of the American, educated and uneducated alike, is abhorrent to the cultured Englishman or Englishwoman, but it is, at any rate, harmonious. That of the Australian is full of discords and surprises. His voice rises and falls with unexpected syncopations, and, even among the few cultured persons this country possesses, seems to bear in every syllable the sign of the parvenu. There is a nouveau riche in culture as well as in material things, and the accent of the cultivated Australian proclaims to the world that his acquisition of learning belongs to his generation alone. At Home, we are occasionally forced to encounter individuals whose sudden access to money is revealed by their tongues, but we are spared from such unpleasant revelations when we meet the intellectuals. These are products of generations. In Australia, they are turned out while you wait, with all the uncouthness of their fathers. Australia alone of all the countries in the world has lingual hobnails on its culture.

In the counties of Great Britain and the provinces of continental Europe the possession of a marked dialect denotes lowly origin. The educated gentleman of Yorkshire or Sligo is differentiated only by a very slight and not displeasing accent. In fact, in Great Britain, the dialect is of some benefit in indicating the origin of the man who uses it. I have frequently found it of value in engaging servants and in dealing with the lower classes generally. But in Australia, this abominable pronunciation pervades the entire continent. The native of Perth and the native of Townsville use precisely the same phrases pronounced precisely the same way, gentleman and labourer alike. Possibly this is one of the results of the extraordinary democracy of this country—a democracy which makes Jack as good as his master. Perhaps it is a cause rather than an effect. When Jack finds his master speaking in the same manner as he does himself, and, making no effort to maintain his position as a gentleman, he is not so much to be blamed for thinking that he is as good as his master—and in Australia he probably is.

The Australian's practice of singing his remarks I can only ascribe to the influence of the Chinese. During my stay in Melbourne, I spent one evening at supper in a Chinese cook-shop in Little Bourke street, and I was instantly struck by the resemblance between the intonation of the phrases passing between the Chinese attendants and that of the conversation of the cultivated Australians who accompanied me. But, in addition to this lack of good-breeding and the gross mispronunciation of common English words, the Australian interlards his conversation with large quantities of slang, which make him frequently unintelligible to the visitor. This use of slang is so common that the public memory forgets that it is slang, and it finds its way into most unexpected places. Chief Justices on their benches, leading newspapers in their editorials, statesmen—such as Australia boasts—all disfigure their utterances by jarring slang terms and phrases, so commonly used as to pass unnoticed by either their hearers or themselves.

English slang has a foundation of humour. There is a note of whimsical comedy about the Oxford undergraduate's practice of calling a bag a bagger, and nobody can repress a smile the first time he hears a coster call eyes "meat-pies" or trousers "round-the-houses." But there is no humour in Australian slang. It is drawn from the lowliest sources—the racecourse, the football match, and the prize-ring. Like most of the imagery of primitive people, it is largely metaphorical, so involved as to require an interpreter.

When a man's chances are regarded as hopeless, the invariable Australian comment is that "he's got Buckley's." After having heard this stupid expression a dozen times, I became curious, and set out on the task of tracing the meaning of it. I ascertained that at the beginning of the nineteenth century three convicts escaped from a party which landed at Port Phillip. Two were killed and eaten by the blacks, but the third, one Buckley, escaped death and lived on friendly terms with the aborigines, to be found alive and well when Melbourne was founded thirty years later. The remote chance of escaping with his life which Buckley secured has since been applied to all remote chances. This is typical of Australian slang, and the visitor who desires to understand fully the patois encountered in this country needs to employ an interpreter.

In conclusion, it is only necessary to point out that so objectionable is the Australian accent that theatrical managers resolutely refuse to employ Australian-born actors or actresses. Though a few of these are possessed of talent—or what passes for talent in Australia—the managers prefer to import English artists of inferior merit, solely because they possess the essential qualifications that Australians lack—the ability to speak the English language.

CHAPTER III.

AUSTRALIAN MANNERS.

Governor King, when in Australia in that administrative capacity, wrote in a despatch of his instituting an orphan school: —

"It is the only step that would ensure some change in the manners of the next generation. God knows this is bad enough."

That was in 1801.

I made diligent search, and that is the last evidence I could find of hope having been entertained for Australian manners.

My observations during the last few months have convinced me that the average Australian simply doesn't know the meaning of the word. One thing that struck me most forcibly is the despicable habit of cadging invitations to the best social functions. I find that it is quite a common thing for a citizen who has been neglected in the case of a big ball to ring up the gentleman in charge of the invitation list, and remind him of the omission. This willingness to humiliate oneself in order to gratify social ambition was a revelation to me. Another thing that left me dumb with astonishment was the boorish behaviour of your women in the trams. I have repeatedly seen an alleged lady compel a man to occupy an uncomfortable seat rather than move up a little to make room for him. A glaring example of this ill-mannered selfishness came under my notice only the other day. A bejewelled female sat on an outside seat with about a foot of spare space on either side of her. A man got in, and jambed himself between her and the end of the seat. The man on the other side of her moved up to allow the society dame to shift along, but not she! She just stuck there, and ignored her unfortunate fellow passenger altogether. It would be difficult to find any country in the older and more cultured world in which the common decencies of civilisation would be so completely ignored.

Nobody ever considers the convenience of others. People in the streets of every civilised portion of the world—I don't say every "other" civilised portion of the world—walk on the right-hand side of the footpath. If one of them happens to be eccentric or possessed of the anti-social instinct or overcome by any cause and obstructs the traffic by walking on the wrong side, he is promptly checked by authority in the guise of a policeman. But in the streets of Sydney there is no such law and order. The public wander over the footpaths like sheep—and with the same directing intelligence. The result is that instead of there being two clearly defined streams of traffic on each footpath there is a struggling, chaotic mass. Under intelligent discipline, and with a people possessed of decent manners, the immense London crowds that fill the streets around the Bank and the Exchange and the Mansion House flow to and fro to their destinations like trains in a railway yard. But in Sydney, where only a comparatively handful of people fill the streets, all is confusion. There being no rule of the path, there is no order. There being no manners, there is no mutual courtesy to ease the position. There being no chivalry, the women get hustled, and the elderly and weak bumped and injured. The police never interfere until somebody is assaulted, and, as may be expected with chaotic traffic regulation and ill-mannered people, this is not an infrequent occurrence. But the moment the offender has been dragged off the police retire to their places by a verandah post, and the same old rabble again fills the footpaths. Considering that the police do not control the vehicles, it is scarcely surprising that they permit the pedestrians to wander where they will. Carts and horses take any course they like. One never hears of anybody being prosecuted for driving on the wrong side of a Sydney street. A London policeman could not believe his eyes were he suddenly transported into an Australian city at a busy hour of the day.

As an example in chaos and ill-manners, the Government provides the public with a tramway system. The tramcars do not run on the wrong side of the road. I'll say that for them. But they commit every other offence against civic management that it is possible to think of. It would be difficult to find any tramways in the world in which the passengers are treated less considerately. The old motto of Boss Tweed, the Tammany leader, was, "The public be damned," and the Government of New South Wales seems to have adopted it for its tramway department. As may be expected, accidents are frequent. It is scarcely possible for anybody who has not visited Australia to picture what this means—a badly managed tramway service, run by badly-mannered officials, and carrying about double the number of badly-mannered passengers. An old time bear-pit must have been a refined assemblage as compared with a Sydney tramcar.

The bad manners of the people are manifest in other places besides the trams and trains and ferries. It is impossible to find a woman who will stand aside to let others in or out of a passage way. One of the most common experiences is to find two or more women standing in front of the turnstile to talk while 50 or 100 persons miss the ferry. The same thing occurs at the doors of all the elevators in places of business, and at the railway wickets. On the tramways, men and women alike rush the doors the moment a car stops, utterly careless of the passengers who wish to alight. In the restaurants customers place parcels, umbrellas, even hats, on the tables. Whether other customers have any elbow room or room for their plates doesn't trouble them one jot. Nobody ever apologises in Australia. One gets used to that after one's toes have begun to get callous from frequent treading on by strange feet. One's dress may be spoilt by a passing painter or by a fellow dancer at a ball overturning a cup of coffee, but one never hears an expression of regret.

The culmination of Australian bad manners was probably reached when the New Year of 1908 was ushered in. Australia on New Year's Eve follows the silly practice of hanging about the streets of the city generally doing nothing. But this time it did something. It let off fireworks. It blew horns and otherwise made a fool of itself. And eventually growing tired of making a fool of itself, it proceeded to make a hog of itself. The women, I understand, were as much to blame as the men at the outset. What followed cannot be related, but the Saturnalia of Ancient Rome, the Bal des Quartz Arts, and the worst of the orgies of seventeenth century rural England all found excellent imitations in the streets of Sydney that night.

CHAPTER IV.

MISS AUSTRALIA.

Everything goes by comparison. If I were unacquainted with England, America, France, Germany and Italy, I might share the delusion cherished by most Australian people—that your women are beautiful. But, having seen the rose, how can I be content with the dandelion?

In accepting the praise of Miss Lily Brayton, your women should remember that this popular actress had a royal time in Australia, and probably was not unmindful of the possibilities of a return visit. No, I am not a disgruntled actress who has found Australian audiences unappreciative of my talent. I am merely a much-travelled woman blessed—or cursed—with the faculty of being able to see things as they really are. When I say that the women to be seen in the streets of Sydney, Melbourne, Adelaide and Hobart are unattractive, I am merely stating the truth as it appeals to me.

Someone with a surprising lack of humour—or an extra large share of it—once wrote of the stately carriage of Australia's matrons and daughters. In my travels in this country the number of women encountered who knew how to walk might be counted on the fingers of one hand. I have seen more grace among the factory girls of Poplar, among the midinettes of the Latin Quarter, and among petticoated toughs of the Bowery, than it has been my fortune to meet in Pitt-street or on the Melbourne Block. Australian women don't walk. Those who don't waddle with an unnatural movement of the hips, like a drake expressing his satisfaction with an extra fat frog, affect a ridiculous mincing gait that resembles nothing so much as the painful perambulation of a youngster who takes off his boots on a hard, pebbly road for the first time.

The best figure I have seen in Australia was that of a young girl of about 18. She was beautifully moulded, with a bust to inspire a poet, and hips of exquisite roundness. Generally speaking, Melbourne women are more favoured in this respect than their Sydney sisters. Here, due possibly to surf-bathing—the bust development is abnormal, while the hips have a flat, board-like appearance. One Sydney woman with rounded hips was introduced to me at tea at the Australia. She was so well formed that I couldn't resist the temptation of testing her genuineness with a hatpin. I don't say that she was padded—I only assert that she took half an inch of steel without flinching!

The best complexions in the Commonwealth are seen at Hobart and Toowoomba—in fact, there seems to be no really pretty skins at any other places. Your women paint and powder too much. The spectacle of young girls of 17 and 18 with rouged cheeks and carmine lips is an absurdity in a country that believes that its women are beautiful.

The new short skirt about to be tried in Paris will never become popular—Australian legs could not be held up to ridicule in that way. It is noteworthy that while in other countries the girl with a pretty ankle and a shapely calf is not unconscious of her charms, the Australian woman is always careful to adjust her skirt on seating herself in tram or train. Why? Because she regards it as immodest to show her legs? The display on the surf beaches disposes of that idea. The answer is found in the fact that, generally speaking, Australian legs are better hidden from view. They are either thick and stocky at the ankles, with a heap of ill-formed flesh above, or are thin almost to the vanishing point. One misses the beautifully-rounded ankles and the graceful tapering calves that peep from beneath petticoats in Bond-street, the Avenue de l'Opera, and Fifth-avenue.

I was amused while at the Hotel Australia one afternoon last week to notice that one "lady," who had evidently studied my first article in the Sydney "Sun," was endeavouring to prove that local legs are worth viewing. Her dress had been carefully adjusted so as to provide a generous display of stocking reaching nearly to the knee. Like so many people in a young country, where the polish and refinement that comes from association with countries in which culture is a much more highly-prized asset, is lacking, she failed to recognise the border line that separates easy naturalness from sheer vulgarity. A woman who pulls up her dress deliberately in order to show her legs is pitifully immodest. The woman who, with malice aforethought, shows her legs is vulgar, and the woman who takes all sorts of trouble to hide them is a prude, but the woman who allows them to be viewed, if the position in which she is seated permits their display, is unaffected and natural. In the society in which I moved in England, France and America, both the women and the men are frankly natural. Here there is, on the one hand, a restraint that is ludicrous, and, on the other hand, a familiarity that is indelicate.

Mr. Norman Lindsay—whose clever work I admired long before I came to this supersensitive Commonwealth—has done me a service in subscribing himself as the man who has seen more of the Australian girl than any of his envious countrymen. If his knowledge is so extensive, and he is the true artist that we all believe him to be, it follows that his drawing must reflect the local type. And what do we find—the grace and beauty over which so many of your frenzied correspondents have rhapsodised? Not on your life. The Norman Lindsay girl is hardly a girl at all. With the calves of a footballer and the upper limbs of a Sandow, she is a fearful and wonderful example of the female form divine. The faces of Mr. Lindsay's women remind me more than anything else of the religious pictures of my youth, designed to represent the torments of hell, and to frighten people into the narrow way. Your foremost black-and-whiter admires the beauty of strength. Well, a draught horse with whiskers half way up its legs is a beautiful thing to draw a heavy load of turnips or road metal, but no one would think of comparing its ungainly proportions with the symmetrical form of the thoroughbred racer. If Australia is trying to breed a race of Amazons, well and good—you are getting along very nicely. But if you are anxious to match your girls with the comelier women of other countries—you have a perfectly clean palette, as my old friend Charles Dana Gibson would put it.

People who read their history closely are familiar with the evolutionary phases through which most young countries pass. Here is first the halting, apologetic stage, represented in the case of Australia by its early-day subservience to England and everything English. Nothing could be any good that was not imported. The next stage was reached when you began to produce a handful of clever men and women, whose success in science, music, art, and sport laid the foundations of a belief that gradually developed into arrogant big-headedness. If Australia could produce a Brennan, a Melba, a Mackennal, a Trumper, an Arnst, and a Gray, why should there be any limit to the fertility of its genius-breeding soil? The idea tickled your vanity, and you allowed it to grow recklessly. People who came from other countries saw your weakness, recognised it as an inevitable phase in your progress towards national sobriety and staidness, and said nice things about you. It made the visitors' stay more pleasant, and, as you will in time grow out of your folly, it helped rather than impeded your development.

Have you ever noticed a puppy let off the chain after being tied up for a long time? He will jump and frisk as though jumping and frisking were the things he was born for, and every time you pat him he bounds a little higher. By-and-bye he begins to feel tired, his tail-wagging becomes less vigorous, and eventually he sits down quietly and wonders why he was silly enough to exert himself so needlessly. He notices, too, that the other dog who watched him with amused tolerance isn't quite such a mongrel as he seemed to be when he gambolled round him; in fact, on closer inspection, he is recognised as being bigger and possessing a shinier coat than his chastened observer. The puppy has learned wisdom. But that pawing and prancing and hind leg foolishness were a necessary part of his education, and every human caress helped him along.

Australia is not yet through the cavorting stage, but it will grow out of it in time, just as other countries have done. If I were an altruist instead of an impartial observer, whose tongue and pen are always guided by clear vision and ripened judgment, I would, I suppose, have helped on the evolutionary process by feeding your vanity with the tablespoonsful doses administered by other visitors. I know I have made myself very unpopular because I wrote the truth as it appealed to me, but we all can't take liberties with our consciences, even to please the women of Australia.

I have been in this country for several months, so that I have had plenty of opportunity of judging the external excellencies of my self-confident southern sisters. The diagrams which I have prepared may help my critics to understand what a perfect figure should look like. The outline of the average Australian woman is shown alongside that of my friend, Miss Maimie Valdervant, of Fifth-avenue, New York. The colonial imperfections are easily distinguishable—the pouter-pigeon breast, the low, flat hips, and the thick, stocky ankles. Miss Valdervant is a beautifully moulded girl, but her shapeliness is not unique. At a weekend party on the Adirondacks at least 10 of the 22 girls present were equally comely. Well do I remember the late Stanford White saying, when someone remarked upon his display of Phidias-chiselled womanhood, that it was nothing unusual. At the Grand Prix meeting at Longchamps Count Pielliet's party was similarly noteworthy; the same thing might be said of the late Viscount Avonmore's famous gathering of 1907, in which I shared with Lady Marjorie Warshane the honor of being the finest figured woman on the lawn.

Who is Valerie Desmond, that she should dare criticise the myriad Venuses of Australia? What does she know of beauty? He who drives fat oxen should himself be fat, and similarly she who writes of the feminine form should have some pretensions to shapeliness herself. I append my measurements for the benefit of my numerous critics:—

The fact that I was asked by the late Sir Edward Poynter to sit for one of his classical studies indicates what a famous artist thought of these proportions.

The reference by one visiting actress who attacked me in the paper to Miss Annette Kellermann's perfection of figure amused me. Everyone in America, if not in Australia, knows how much of her popularity is due to beauty and how much to her press agent. Your clever and jolly water nymph is anything but well balanced. Her legs are—or were when I last saw them—much too thin for her superb bust. It is just the reverse with Miss Pansy Montague (La Milo). The upper half of her spoils an otherwise beautiful figure. The genius of Cruikshank—an Australian of whom, in his own particular line, his country has reason to be proud—makes amends for this deficiency. He was able to convince the English public that La Milo was one of the most beautiful women living, and the habit of admiring her became general. I remember drawing Mr. W.T. Stead's attention to her comparatively puny bust, but so completely had Cruikshank gulled him that he wouldn't hear a word against her.

It is not difficult to understand why Australian women should regard themselves as beautiful. You know the Papuan natives who stain their teeth with betel nut think white molars hideous. When any country sets up its own style of beauty it takes a good while to convince it that any other style can be beautiful, let alone to force the admission that the local gods are false. So few Australians have travelled that a restricted horizon is natural. I don't say that your women have anything to be ashamed of in having abnormal busts, flat hips, and thick ankles, but when they arrogate to themselves the right to set up a standard for the world I really must protest.

CHAPTER V.

AUSTRALIA FOR THE AUSTRALIANS.

This watchword is the motto of "the national newspaper." It is also the top note of all the Labour party screeches.

The national weakness of Australia it shows is instinctive. There is a distrust of its own capability; self-reliance is totally absent; there is no vital growth.

Never was the confirmation of such wretched defects in a people so complete as in this confessional clamour, this lack of combating power of pride of race.

Ostensibly it is to exclude inferiors, but it really argues against the incoming of superiors. In striking contrast is it from the "Let 'em all come" policy of Great Britain.

The screaming farce of the whole business, however, is the education test immigrants are subjected to. They must be able to write a line of some European language. Why, official figures show that there are in Australia nearly 400,000 persons over the usual literate age who cannot read and write.

"Australia for the Australians" is merely the cowardice shriek, "Preservation for the incompetent." To exclude is to fear, disguised howsoever it be.

Such widespread self-deceit as to its being anything else is impossible of credence. It is the craven state of pampered workers that has infected all classes in Australia. Periodically the country gets an attack of delirium tremens, and then it sees the black man, the yellow man, and variegated mankind generally with the upper hand.

And this is the hysterical way it then acts (vide a Brisbane paper):—

"ALIENS CAN'T LAND.
NOT EVEN TO BE BURIED.
A CUSTOMS DISCOVERY.

"A colored man named L. Peraira, second cook on the B.I.S.N. Company's steamer Onipenta, now berthed at the A.U.S.N. Company's Norman Wharf, died on board the vessel on Wednesday evening. Deceased had been attended by a doctor, who certified that death was due to heart failure caused by beri-beri. Under the circumstances the usual certificate was issued, and arrangements made for the burial of the body. Particulars of the death reached the Customs authorities in due course, and it is stated they took exception to the landing of the body for interment, and claimed that they were acting in conformity with the terms of the Alien Immigration Restriction Act. By the time this attitude of the Customs authorities became known, the undertaker had, it is said, completed his work, and the body of the deceased had been interred. It now remains to be seen what further action, if any, the authorities will take in the matter."

In the meantime the rich tropical lands are given over to rank growths, and are referred to for the purposes of borrowing and peroration as the "great national resources of Australia."

When the Japanese squadron was in Australian waters, the Admiral confided in the commanding officer of the Commonwealth forces that both his country and China had envious eyes cast upon these self-same tropical tracts. If it were not for the protection Great Britain affords Australia there would be very little to stop either yellow Power from materialising its envy. The Japanese squadron told Australia plainly what it thought of its coastal defences just as an indication of all this. Great precaution had been taken not to allow any camera parties from the Japanese boats over the fortifications when in the port of Melbourne. The Japs simply went and looked round casually. But when they fired their farewell salute just without the "Heads" the squadron hove-to at a spot where it could shell Queenscliff while not one gun in those fortifications could be brought to bear on it. And just at present we have the spectacle of a party of Japanese explorers encamped within sight of Sydney's main fortifications.

When Australia works itself into a cold perspiration about the yellow man, it, ipso facto, acknowledges the equality of him. The same with the nigger who is, at the most, only wanted to do the lowest form of tropical field work. But it is the custom of the demagogues in Australia to talk about "the dignity of labour" without discrimination of any kind.

For the Indian coolie, say, to be able to do given work at a less wage than a white, at the same time doing it better, surely gives him some claim to be considered in the economic scheme of things. Then take the ethical point of view. The coolie lives a less brutal life than the great proportion of northern white workers, and shows a greater margin of savings out of a lesser wage. He is thus emphatically more desirable than the aforesaid proportion of Australian white worker, which has no margin out of wages after paying for beer, but usually has the next week's wages mortgaged to the local publican.

For it is only the wreckage, the scum of the stream of life that drift to tropical field labour. When I went among them I felt for the first time the shame of the comparison of those of my own race with the South Sea nigger.

Better fence the nigger into Australia and deport the white who has sunk so low as to take coolie work to some country where they have not laws against undesirable immigrants. Australia is the only country where the white is consumed with that ignoble desire.

"But," shrieks the Labour agitator, "the Australian spends his money and is better for the community."

Personally, I have scant sympathy and no admiration for the fat-fingered publican and his brother (by trade ties) the brewer.

The same objection was taken to the coolie as is taken to the Chinaman—viz., he is saving and economic. And if good citizenship is merely a matter of spending money with the beer vendor—plainly a false and untenable premise—then was the Kanaka of all "desirables" the most to be desired. All he got out of the production of a ton of sugar, valued at £20, roughly, was 30/-, and at that cost he created a profitable avenue of energy for the white worker. He never took a shilling back to his island.

The American is getting over "the dignity of labour" trouble by machinery. The Australian hasn't the brains to do likewise, nor is he a workman as reliable as a mechanical contrivance, because the latter doesn't get drunk or strike on any pretext.

CHAPTER VI.

THE AUSTRALIAN IN SOCIETY.

There is no work for the phrase noblesse oblige to do in Australia. The nearest one can get to it is noveau riche. For in Australia the parvenu is paramount.

The people have no ancestry to boast of; all its nastiness is near the surface. If it isn't the beer pump half the time I am very much mistaken.

For the other half history is not silent. Arthur Gayle tells of it in the "Bulletin's" History of Botany Bay. Not so very long ago he wrote: "We are still ridden by the influence and ruled by the lineal descendants of the squalid officialdom of the grisly past. The whistle of the lash and the clank of the convict's chain are still distinctly heard though fifty years have passed away since transportation ceased. The reason is, in a word, that the men of the class that came into existence under the Imperial regime made the most of their time. They founded family fortunes and became territorial magnates, the lords of the soil...."

But it was not only "squalid officialdom" that made the most of its time. Those comprising the other class were also "in the van of circumstance."

"Be thou therefore in the van of circumstances,

Yea, seize the arrow's barb."—Keats.

They had in England been in a different kind of van—Black Maria. Subsequently they got the "Arrow's barb"—broad arrows. The genealogical records have been destroyed, but ever and anon the grim figure in prison garb steps out of the family cupboards. Sometimes it is mere atavism. During the visit of the American Fleet all the spoons were stolen from the Flagship during a reception. Again, when Shackleton returned from his Antarctic exploration Esquimo dogs were stolen from the Nimrod. Last time, however, that fifty thousand or so close-cropped heads obtruded themselves through the interstices of family cupboard doors it was at the beck of Lord Beauchamp, who is an Australian. He duly qualified as such by making a general Australian of himself when Governor of New South Wales. His first act of bad tact and worse taste was to send this little

Kipling slur over the telegraph wire to Sydney by way of showing that they must regard him as one of themselves:—

"Greeting! my birthstains have I turned to good;Forcing strong wills perverse to steadfastness;The first flush of the tropics in my blood,And at my feet success."

It showed an appreciative, social spirit—that sort of Australian spirit that leads to calling each other names, etc., at meals.

The next proof of his being an Australian was for him to deny, through one Henry Lawson, that he sent the slur. A friend of mine, however, has seen the "birthstains" message in his handwriting, and, furthermore, knows where it now is.

But tuft-hunting Sydney society obligingly pushed the close-cropped heads back inside the cupboards and tried to marry their daughters to the Australian who had caused their ancestors to feel restive to the point of obtrusiveness.

As he became more and more Australian, Lord Beauchamp made a delicate concession to society snobbery. He issued blue and white tickets when he entertained. It was a nice differentiation of the status of his guests. Seidlitz-powder functions they were called, but the recipients of both blue and white went for all the disturbing elements.

And the matrons still pursued Lord Beauchamp with their daughters. Eventually they ran him out of the country.

As is usual with Australians, once he went to England little more was heard of him. He married there, however—that, of course, was cabled, and Australian snob papers have since had domestic details, including the birth and christening.

Whenever I have felt sympathetic with Australia it has been on the score of what it has to put up with from the cable man and the London correspondent. She can't shake off her old Governors, and she also has the relatives of those in gubernatorial state inflicted upon her. For instance, when Lord Brassey was falling out of, off, and under things in Victoria, an additional family misfortune was cabled. His brother, while playing tennis, was hit in the eye with a ball. Victorian society liked it; it gave the opportunity to write condolences and have the Government House orderly ride up to its front door and leave the acknowledgment.

When the Australian pater-vulgarius makes a rise in the world his daughters start to teach him etiquette. If he blows his nose in the way we expect Gabriel will announce himself one of these mornings early, it is "bad form," and he may not even know his friends of adversity. Fortune makes him acquainted with well-fed fellows—at his own board—to whom he is most affable. If he would keep silent and let his money do the talking his daughters would be less fidgety. It must be an awful thing to try to regulate one's behaviour by a book on etiquette, and, but for his bound and hide, the torture of the new-rich Australian with a family would be worse than vivisection. But he has bound and hide. God is good to him.

But the family take the altered circumstances seriously. They become finickety on the matter of social distinctions. Had their father kept a shop they cease to remember the fact, and shopkeepers in general are altogether "beyond." So is now also the reception of a suburban mayoress. For has not the head of the house been made an M.L.C., bringing them into contact with vice-royalty. It is as often as not of the slightest, but the newspapers only publish a list of "those present."

It is the same when these women are gathered together ostensibly in charity's cause. Charity begins at snobbery in Australia. Let the wife of a Governor but take the chair, and the institution in need of funds is "deserving" from the moment the announcement goes forth.

Max O'Rell saw it all. Hear what he said: "Colonial society has absolutely nothing original about it. It is content to copy all the shams, all the follies, all the impostures of the old British world. You will find in the Southern Hemisphere that venality, adoration of the golden calf, hypocrisy and cant are still more noticeable than in England, and I can assure you that a badly cut coat would be the means of closing more doors upon you than would a doubtful reputation." This was really another way of saying Australia is a land of doubtful reputations.

Everybody in Australian society is better than everybody else, and everybody can give full and particular reasons why (including dates). The position is obvious—everybody is trying to hide what everybody else knows, and is prepared to make even better known should occasion offer.

This is a natural consequence of money being the "open sesame." It does not matter how the money may have been acquired. The sons and daughters of pawnbrokers, for example, loom large in Melbourne society to-day. And butchers become squatters. This, above all, the money must have been made; society starts the nouveaux riches from that point. Money covers everything—except the women at evening entertainments.

CHAPTER VII.

THE AUSTRALIAN AT SHIRK.

The masterly inactivity of the Australian is something to marvel at. He is, of course, very tired, but how he manages to get along without doing any kind of work from early morn to dewy eve throughout the circle of the golden year I must confess knocks me kite high. It's not that he dislikes work. He is really very fond of it—in the abstract.

This is borne out by an account of Sydney business methods published in an evening paper of that city in the form of an extract from a commercial traveller's diary. It is most illustrative:—

"MONDAY.—Called to see Mr. Beeswax, of the firm of Beeswax and Bullswool, in the hope of placing a big line of saddlers' ironmongery with him. Mr. Beeswax sent out word that he wanted something of the sort, but that, being Monday, he was busy clearing up business left over from the Saturday half-holiday. Asked me to call again.

"TUESDAY.—Called again. Mail day. Mr. Beeswax couldn't see me. To call to-morrow.

"WEDNESDAY.—English mail arrived late, and letters only to hand to-day. Mr. Beeswax busy with English letters. To call to-morrow.

"THURSDAY.—Called again. Mr. Beeswax gone to Arbitration Court to fight his employees. May be in again; may not. Most likely not! I went to the Arbitration Court and waited. Beeswax was fined £100 for selling wooden dolls and toothpicks in contravention of the 951st clause of the Amalgamated Wooden Dolls and Toothpick Makers' Union log. I decided not to approach him for an order to-day.

"FRIDAY.—Called again just before twelve. Cab was waiting outside. Just as I was shown into the room, Mr. Beeswax was putting on his hat. I said, 'About that saddlers' ironmongery!' He said, 'D—— your saddlers' ironmongery! Who won the toss, did you hear?' Then he jumped into a cab, and said, 'Cricket Ground!' and drove off.

"SATURDAY.—Only half a day. No hope of seeing Beeswax, or anyone else for that matter. Decided to go to the Cricket Ground myself and join the crowd whose prosperity during the week enables them to enjoy themselves on Saturday free from care. I have no cares—no money either. Next week there is a public holiday for the election, a levee, and another cricket match, so I don't suppose I shall sell much saddlers' ironmongery just for a while. Australia is such a busy place."

The only thing I doubt about this is the persistence of the commercial traveller. I have seen a good deal of that flamboyant person in my travels of Australia, and the conclusion I formed of him was that he was not out to do business so much as to circulate the latest risque story, criticise the management of railways and hotels, explain the European situation, and generally to make the rustic gape and feel discontented. He is the great Australian "bounder."

Every Australian who isn't in the Civil Service aspires to be a business man. Art and matters of temperament are side lines, so to speak. Primarily, it is the business faculty that is developed in all lie-downs of Australian life. It is generally as office boy that a start is made. The position of office boy means that young Australia is paid ten shillings per week to look through the "situations vacant" column in his employer's paper every morning, and apply for all positions advertised at 15s. per week by other firms, said applications to be written on his employer's notepaper. If he doesn't get another place quickly he knows he'll be sacked, for nobody keeps an office boy in Australia more than a week. Indeed, his record has been sung in verse thus harmoniously:—

Monday, hired;Tuesday, tired;Wednesday, fired.

One week you see the business man in the making a messenger at a chemist's shop. Next week he is carrying reporters' "copy" from meetings to the sub-editor of an evening paper. The week after that he is taking tickets at a picture show. The following week he will be delivering circulars down drain pipes. Then he will put in two days sweeping up the hair about barbers' chairs in a saloon and brushing customers up to the level of the elbows where the bits of hair are not. He will next take a spell at driving a cart, and after that go bill posting at night. At this work he will become acquainted with a theatrical manager, and will abandon it to go on with the populace in melodrama until he gets a job working a lift. He is by this time a fully qualified clerk. At the age of twenty he applies for admission to the police force. All Australians do that, apparently under the belief that it's the only position that will enable them to keep out of gaol.

At twenty-five the Australian thinks it's about time he fixed on some occupation. "I have had a large and varied experience," he now writes when applying for a billet. It is immaterial to him what appointments are offering; he answers the lot. He will manage a station or a tea-house or take a private secretaryship to a Minister of the Crown or test eyesight for an optician. He doesn't mind taking the message to Garcia—not he. He likes it to be by way of a racehorse, however.

When he's fixed up in an occupation he thinks will suit him, the Australian gets the sack. His employer finds him absolutely useless. He has not the habit of industry, and he is incapable of sustained effort of any kind. Ask him (if he is in a produce firm) the price of butter as quoted in that morning's paper, and he won't know. But he can give you the betting card at Tatt.'s without hesitation. He is indifferent to everything connected with the business of his employer. He knows that if the worse comes to the worse he can sleep out.

Australians who think of going to another country with the idea of making a sleepihood should inquire fully as to the climate.

CHAPTER VIII.

THE LISTLESS POLICEMAN.

The Australian policeman never knows anything; it's no use asking him the time even.

This gives some idea of police protection, and what goes on in Australia: —

"SENSATIONAL ROBBERY.

"£600 WORTH OF

GOLD

STOLEN FROM A POLICE STATION.

"The Inspector-General of Police has been notified by the Superintendent at Albury that a sensational robbery has occurred at Tumberumba, in New South Wales, and that something between £500 and £600 worth of gold dust and retorted gold had been stolen from the local police station."

And from the same paper the same week: —

"WHILE THE CONSTABLE SLEPT.

"At an early hour this morning the house of Constable — —, a constable attached to Redfern Station, was broken into. The constable had gone on duty at an early hour in the morning, and about 3 in the afternoon went to bed in his residence at Young-street, the other members of his family having gone out. Everything was properly secured, and it did not enter the constable's head that anyone would have the hardihood to break into his premises. Some time between 4 and 5 o'clock, he got up, and went downstairs, and was astonished to find that the house had been broken into and robbed while he slept. Entrance had been effected by the kitchen window, the woodwork of which had been smashed."

The Australian criminal is the most clumsy scoundrel in creation. He leaves enough clues behind him for a jury to get to work on right away. But unless he happens to leave his name and address a cracksman working on a fair sized crib is never caught. Most murderers, with the exception of those who gave themselves up, are at large in Australia. This last remark does not refer to cases of murder followed by the suicide of the perpetrator. A list of the undetected crimes of Australia would cost too much to print.

CHAPTER IX.

THE AUSTRALIAN'S PARASITICAL TENDENCIES.

The Australian is a born loafer. Go you north, south, east, or west in his mortgaged land, and in proportion to the distance you travel, so does this truth broaden upon you – the truth of his loafing propensities.

He is also a parasite. The big Australian parasite feeds smaller parasites, and so ad infinitum.

Nationally the Australian has been a borrower by choice. He is the spendthrift, ne'er-do-well, who is always a drain on the old man's purse. He has from the start been getting remittances from John Bull in the guise of loans, which, like Micawber, he redeems by more loans.

He has the borrowing habit bad.

The result?

If the Australian wants to develop something, a mine, say, he makes a bee line to the member of Parliament for the district, and through his pernicious office enough is squeezed out of the milch-cow government to sustain him until he can hawk what he has round London. He seldom has any money himself, and when he has he prefers not to risk it. The role of promoter suits him best. He gets his profits out of his flotation, and impudently stands in with the "paid-ups." As often as not this latter trick is to give verisimilitude to his bona fides.

His name is associated with the untamed feline on the London market just now.

His private ideas about finance are reflected in public accounts, particularly in the States that have local government or irrigation boards. Sufficient is it here to indicate his trend and point the baneful influence – the antithesis of exalting to the country.

There is said to be honour among thieves, and on the prima facie case thus made out, I cannot bring myself to call the Australian business man a thief. Americans have a term for a despised class of their community, "Suckers" they call those who comprise it. In its worst sense the term fits the

Australian. Wherever some sporadic energy is exhibited, there do you find the suckers.

The sucker is chiefly found in big cities built on borrowed money and by boom swindles. Thither flock all who have foresworn honest toil, and the disinclination to work, as has been already observed, is innate of the Australian.

The sucker fastens on industry wherever it is to be found, and if a district threatens to thrive, a big town full of suckers arises to drain the profits, and thus is the producer, who, in Australia, economically is the country, impoverished. He and the primary industries never get a chance. Things are foisted upon him that he does not want and is not in a position to pay for, and he can't move without giving some sucker a commission. The commission is generally for doing something, which, if he had any sense, which he hasn't, the producer could do for himself. So it happens that cities and towns are over populated by suckers, who buy drinks for the producer with the latter's money, and do ditto for him who purchases what has been produced (drinks again at the producer's expense).

And all this the reprehensible politician merely calls centralisation. If he were less reprehensible, he would acquaint himself with the state of things and then set about remedying them. The figures would astound a statesman. Think of it: the population of the Commonwealth was last census 3,773,248, and 47 towns absorbed 1,859,313 of the number! The increase per cent. of the population, further, was only 1.71, while the cities are continuously absorbing the rural dwellers. "Debts," remarks Coghlan, "have grown at a much more rapid pace than population."—[Statistical Account of Australia.]

The sucker curse is daily becoming more acute in Australia. It so happens that the young Australian whose father is trying to make a farmer of him registers a resolution that he will be a sucker. With justification, no doubt, he regards his father as a fool. (All Australians regard their fathers as fools.) The fool-farmer's son starts his sucking, therefore, as a commission agent, and goes on the election committee of the surplus Australian politician standing in the "country interest," and whose watchword is "settle the people on the land." The sucker certainly does his best to settle the people on the land, but not in the sense that the humourless politician utters the shibboleth.

CHAPTER X.

THE AUSTRALIAN'S LACK OF PATRIOTISM.

It so happens that the Australian couldn't, even if he wanted to, say, "This is my own, my native land." That is, of course, with any degree of truth. For the Australian has long since put the country in pawn.

Instead of evincing any lofty sentiment, however, the Australian is generally to be heard cursing his country, and a good number of him get away from it the first opportunity the good God gives them. And small wonder. It is a land of burlesque. It is built on entirely wrong principles. The mountains are all round the coast, and they keep the rain from going inside. The consequence is that there is always a drought in the interior, which same remark applies also to the Australian himself.

"It's a good place to live out of," says the ignominious Australian, if you ask him anything about it.

In his dunderheadedness he can't see that he has fenced out enterprise, and is fast legislating himself out of the country. The emigration figures of Australia represent those of the inhabitants who can scrape a couple of hundred pounds together in order to escape the national debt, the suckers, and the reprehensible politician.

When it was proposed that Australia should borrow the money in England to give England a Dreadnought, one of the State Premiers was interviewed on the subject. He sounded the depths in patriotic sentiment by remarking, "It would be a good advertisement!"

It is only in a Mr. Alfred Deakin peroration or that of some other silver-tongue that you hear of Australian patriotism. Silver tongue, by the way, is a mere euphemism; there is a more direct and much shorter Saxon synonym.

If Australia were a great country, it would have the natural corollary, a great man. But it has never produced one.

Sir Henry Parkes once proposed to erect a mausoleum for the illustrious dead of Australia, but the hopelessness of getting eligible corpses caused the idea to be abandoned. There are, however, in Australia many unexplained monuments. Among the latest was one in Brisbane, raised to a deceased Rugby football player. Will the Australian ever get any sort of sense of proportion?

But a people, I suppose, must first of all have love of country before it gets a standard of measurement. If a plebiscite were taken it would be found that the memory of Edward Kelly is far more revered by the citizens of this mean country than that of any other citizen. This national hero was familiarly known as Ned Kelly. After a series of misunderstandings with the police, he died suddenly one morning.

The individual Australian, be it here remarked, does not consider the collective Australian much class, and the Australian who has travelled has a sneaking disregard for his compatriots. If he has spent two months in London, he returns an ape Englishman. So far as loose clothes and cheap mannerisms will carry him he is a Londoner. It is a noticeable fact that he imitates the most inane of insular types. The more howling the particular London ass of the period, the more sincere the Australian flattery of him. This needs no comment.

And when this two-months-in-England idiot returns to Australia some gushing she-Australian will say to him—

"Oh, Mr. Absent Two-Months (Printer, don't forget the hyphen), I can tell you're an Englishman. You're so different from the Australian."

At this Mr. Absent Two-Months will smile smugly, conscious of the higher appraisement.

Then he will commend her for her discernment in words.

"Well—er, I was born out he—ah," he will say, "But, you know, I—er have lived in England—haw!"

She just dotes on Englishmen. She likes the way they turn their trousers up at the bottoms.

Then they start. He will agree with her in sweeping depreciation of Australia and all who live in it, and he will tell her what a jolly country

England is. She will sigh sympathetically to the cad, instead of calling in the dust-bin emptier to pole-axe him. It would be a more patriotic extreme.

Now how could this kind of woman kindle the spark of patriotism in her children, assuming for the moment that she was prepared to bear them? How could she instil love of country? She has no passion for things Australian. Her mother never adopted the country for a start. She was one of those wistful creatures who called Old England "Home," and her children learnt it right enough.

And these Australian women are now lending a voice in the country's affairs. The word voice is used deliberately. It is about the only thing the Australian will lend the country.

CHAPTER XI.

CLUB LIFE IN AUSTRALIA.

I've been assured by fellow countrymen exiled in this land that if you take an Australian into your club he'll put his hand in his pocket and ask you what you will have to drink. That, of course, is just a little demonstration, meaning that he feels perfectly at home.

The Australian clubs take on all sorts of names, but the same atmosphere pervades the lot. In some clubs are men who have been members for years who couldn't tell you where the reading-room was. They only know the way to the bar.

But to return to the atmosphere of Australian clubs, I am assured by friends that it is engendered of a rank and common suspicion that one member is going to endeavour to borrow money from another. One feels the constraint in the air at once, and no one gets jolly and hilarious in consequence, but just "cunning" drunk. A man can't escape the borrower in Australia—and he gauges the standing of a club by the magnitude of the loan a member suggests.

A visitor to an Australian club can never be sure as to whom he is going to meet. If a tailor happens to be in a fair way of business he probably makes the members of some club feel uncomfortable every time a glass door swings open. Pinero said something derogatory about solicitors in clubs. They're in all Australian clubs. I have heard of a solicitor taking revenge out of an Australian who had been dodging service of a writ, issued from the said solicitor's office, for weeks. But the Australian guessed the boy with the writ was on the pavement and evaded the solicitor's stare by putting a comic paper between him and it. One also meets the dentist in most Australian clubs.

Some of the developments of the literary club are peculiar to Australia. For example, on the selection committee of the Johnsonian Club, Brisbane, is a man whose greatest literary effort was the announcement to a gasping audience that "There were no cases set down for hearing at the Police Court this morning." In the same club are many who could not tell you who

Boswell was any more than some members of the Melbourne Yorick could tell you what Hamlet killed behind the arras. If you asked after midnight the most literary of them they would, as one voice, say, "A blood-red mouse."

I have been at some loss to know what makes a person eligible for membership at one of the many Australian city clubs. But enquiry has brought to light some "pilling" episodes. I have known a father pilled for membership of a club and his son go through all right. But the father had educated the son up as a snob. He dressed better than his governor and sponged on him. I have often wondered if the old chap knew what a compliment the members of the club paid him in deciding he was not fit to associate with his son.

The languid swell element has invaded all Australian clubs. Publicans' sons most do congregate in them when people who work for a living are out after a crust. These youths take mental exercise reading the theatrical gossip and social columns of the weekly snob papers. They are walking encyclopædias of useless information, and may be trusted to make fools of themselves on all occasions.

They experience a great joy in pointing out to foolish little girls in the street a man in the public eye as So-and-So, "a honorary member of our club." So-and-So, probably an imported actor, however, is blissfully unaware of his advertiser's existence.

These Australian clubs metaphorically tumble over each other to have a distinguished visitor to toady to, and to get a little of the reflected glory they will sign chits for his drinks till all's blue, if he happens to be sufficiently hoggish to keep pace with them.

In the absence of any intellectual powers, the Australian clubman's idea of thoroughly entertaining a guest is to get drunk with him. To put a man to bed—take his boots off and all that—is the height of his hospitality.

Some Australians in their cups to-day will wax reminiscent on the days when "the nights we used to have at the old Bandicoot Club."

There is an expression in Australia, "Blind as a bandicoot." It's at variance with natural history, but most sayings are in conflict with fact in Australia. Truth there dwells at the bottom of an artesian bore.

CHAPTER XII.

THE AUSTRALIAN ON THE LAND.

The man on the land in Australia is represented by two classes, the squatter and the cockatoo farmer. Why the latter is so called I am at a loss to know. He never has a feather to fly with. The squatter is more birdlike. He puts on a lot of "wing," and some of him go so far as to flout a crest.

Many of the squatters of to-day in Australia are the descendants of cattle "duffers," as their nondescript herds amply testify. A fine portly legislator of the present time has a couple of well-stocked stations, and generally looms large in Australian landscape. One day, before he became smug, a neighbour of his caught him with an unbranded calf in his yard, and cried, "Heigh! That calf is not yours!" "No," he called back, "but it will be as soon as the iron is hot!"

I wouldn't like to be an Australian squatter for many reasons. That is, of the old type. There are a few importations of recent years—men with clean breeding and clean money—from England. They're all right. But they are not representative of the class. As a class squatters are illiterate, and an exemplification of the poet's mock logic that "The man who drives fat cattle must himself be fat"—particularly about the head. They are used chiefly as members of the different Legislative Councils, where they obstruct liberal land laws with much vehemence and bad grammar. They are in the main responsible for the slow settlement of Australian agricultural lands by their relentless harassment of the selector at every point. The result is a trend towards land monopolies. New South Wales illustrates the case. The evidence and finding of the Lands Scandals Commission showed that a Minister of the Crown in New South Wales accepted enormous bribes to perpetuate this state of things; there have also been land scandals in Victoria and Queensland. In that State 24 men or companies hold 44 million acres between them, and hold this preposterous area so tightly that when Australians complain that it is unfair to judge the country's indebtedness on a population basis they should remember that this sort of thing debars immigration: it rather accentuates the borrowing plight, by causing emigration.

The squatter encourages pests, not people, to settle on the land. It was a squatter who introduced sparrows into Australia, and rabbits, and Scotch thistles, and docks, and the bot fly; also swine fever. A squatter's son is a chip off the old blockhead. When he's about twenty he's sent to England for a brush up, and he either becomes an absentee or returns to help make Australian cities more vicious. As a rule he acquires a beautifully discriminative taste for whisky, and what time he is sober races horses on the most approved spieling method. There was one of him in the Sydney Equity Court recently, who said he had been drunk for eight years, and that the whole of that time was a blank to him.

The evening papers chronicled how many times he had delirium tremens, and how many times he had fits, and how as Vicar's warden he took up the collection in the country church and breathed whisky fumes on the congregation. He sat on the Bench—drunk: he played polo—drunk: he was captain of a volunteer corps—drunk: he read family prayers—drunk: he started races—drunk: he sat on the hospital committee—drunk: when he couldn't do these things he was dead—drunk.

But to the cockatoo. There is little to be said of him. He spends most of his time growling. He would have you believe that his title deeds are in a lawyer's office in perpetuity as security for loans, while the local grocer invariably has a lien over his crops. He is, as a matter of fact, mostly well to do, but the way he lives it is to be hoped will never in its sordidness be known to the other half of the world. His wail for cheap railway freights and seed wheat ceaseth not, and though he has learnt to call himself the backbone of the country he is really a national calamity. In the back country he is little better than his dog.

Francis Adams says his heathenism is intense, and that everyone in the bush is at heart a pessimist. He has almost lost the power of speech, and his jaws move with difficulty when he attempts it. Henry Lawson, an Australian, tells of the intelligence of the bushman at his highest development in a study entitled "His Colonial Oath." He writes: I recently met an old schoolmate of mine up country. He was much changed. He was tall and lank, and had the most hideously bristly red beard I ever saw. He was working on his father's farm. He shook hands and looked anywhere but in my face, and said nothing. Presently I remarked at a venture:

"So poor old Mr. B., the school master, is dead?"

"My oath!" he replied.

"He was a good sort?"

"My oath!"

"Time goes pretty quickly, doesn't it?"

"His oath (colonial)."

"Poor old Mr. B. died awfully sudden, didn't he?"

He looked up the hill and said, "My oath!"

Then he added: "My blooming oath!"

I thought my perhaps city rig or manner embarrassed him, so I stuck my hands in my pockets, spat, and said, so as to set him at his ease: "It's blanky hot to-day. I don't know how you blanky blanks stand such blank weather. It's blanky well blank enough to roast a crimson carnal bullock, ain't it?" Then I took out a cake of tobacco, bit off a quarter, and pretended to chew. He replied:

"My oath!"

The conversation flagged here. But presently, to my great surprise, he came to the rescue with:

"He finished me, you know?"

"Finished? How? Who?"

He looked down towards the river, thought (if he did think) and said: "Finished me edyercation, yer know!"

"Oh! you mean Mr. B.?"

"My oath!—he finished me first-rate."

"He turned out many good scholars, didn't he?"

"My oath! I'm thinkin' about going down to the training school!"

"You ought to—I would if I were you."

"My oath!"

"Those were good old times," I hazarded. "You remember the old bark school?"

He looked away across the siding, and was evidently getting uneasy. He shifted about and said: "Well, I must be going."

"I suppose you're pretty busy now?"

"My oath! So long!"

"Well, good-bye. We must have a yarn some day."

"My oath!"

He got away as quickly as he could....

The Australian bushman has, what is generally known as a "rat"; in fact, the lunacy of Australia is most alarming. "There seems little doubt that insanity is slowly but steadily increasing in the States," remarks Coghlan, on the Commonwealth. He is only working on the figures asylum returns show. If only the idiots of the backblocks were included, the mad rate per thousand in Australia—now in excess of that of England—would stagger humanity.

CHAPTER XIII.

THE AUSTRALIAN TITLED PERSON.

Everyone in Australia is in imminent peril of a title. Nobody is safe. There is no saying whose turn it will be next. When he gets up in the morning the first thing the Australian does is to look at the paper and see if his name is among the list of those knighted or otherwise decorated. The distribution seems to run like a sweep consultation. So many K.C.M.G.'s, so many C.M.G.'s, and so on. Then they put the names of all the people of Australia into a hat and draw for them.

There is no other way of explaining how the people who have titles got them, or why. In only one instance on record is there a proper fit. It is the particular case of a Sydney publican who sells threepenny beers with a free "counter lunch." He was made a C.M.G. The humour of the lottery once more. It is most amusing to anybody from the old country to see funny little men "Sirred" in Australia.

People whose luck is so much out that they can't draw a title make shift in the meantime with a hyphen. It is just as well that strangers know this for the purposes of answering invitations. Never forget the hyphen in Australia. No "family" is without it. In the early days Brown was hyphenated to Smith with a gyve.

The Australian titled person is mostly under-educated and over-fed. He is of no particular use except to company promoters, who put his name on the front page of a prospectus. Sometimes he opens a bazaar. He prefers, however, eating at complimentary banquets tendered to anybody whose fellow townsmen think justifies a gorge.

The prodigality with which the people responsible hand out titles to Australians is no doubt part of the scheme which sprang from the mind of William Charles Wentworth, the originator in the country of "that fatal drollery called representative government." Wentworth was known as "the shepherd king"—the titular craze again. There was also in Australia a bushranger king. Hall, who was shot by a policeman, was so titled by the

New South Wales Premier of the times, Hon. (afterwards, of course, Sir) John Robertson. Hall owned a station.

But to return to Wentworth's scheme. It was to found "a colonial aristocracy," a House of Peers—"a replica of England rather than America." Martin in his "Australia and the Empire" chronicles the folly. "The subject," he wrote, "had been for years maturing in his (Wentworth's) mind; he even expounded his views on this question of an Australian House of Lords in a long-forgotten article in the pages of an English magazine...." Yet on this point of creating a brand new colonial aristocracy he failed miserably. The commonest street orator in Sydney could raise a ready laugh by giving a list of the expectant "nobility." Robert Lowe opposed it in the House of Commons, and his criticism had all the weight of colonial experience, while a young Sydney tradesman, by name Henry Parkes, as Dr. Lang described the Premier of New South Wales, first rose to public notoriety and favour by his diatribes against this feature of Wentworth's great measure.

The young Sydney tradesman afterwards drew a knighthood himself, and didn't send it back to the title lottery department of the Colonial Office.

There are certain fat people in Australia who are scant of breath through pursuing the House of Lords' will-o'-the-wisp. Desperate have been the efforts exerted.

The progeny of the innumerable crop of pompous low-order knights and colonial-made Gentlemen in Australia does not benefit to any enviable degree. Living up to a hyphen is bad enough, but when it comes to an order it invariably means an inheritance of debts, ending in passe daughters becoming manicurists (an occupation not respectable since the gay Lord Quex), and the sons up-country police-court practitioners, or £100-a-year civil servants. On even footing with the low-order knights are the "honourables." They approximate to Wentworth's House of Peers, membership of State Legislative Councils carrying the title. The "honourables" guinea-pig mainly for a living. The title also means Government House entree, and rating at functions where there is recourse to precedence. Wives and daughters thus get their hands on the social lever, and so, later on, catch, with great adroitness, the overworked reception smile of Governors' clever consorts. Clever because it must often be so hard to refrain from laughing outright.

I should like to share some of the fun at the various Government Houses after a reception.

It is rather rough on them, though, not to be able to enjoy the comedy while it is in progress. Seldom can they. There is, however, a time on record when they did to the full—so did many others who had a "Burke's Peerage" on their library shelves. The Duke of Buccleugh was cabled to have sailed for Australia. "A title!" cried some. "A Duke!" gasped other Australians. Society was agog. But it was only a very well-bred bull shipped for stud purposes.

Is it any wonder that "the commonest street orator" can raise a laugh when Australian titles are mentioned?

CHAPTER XIV.

THE AUSTRALIAN AT THE BREAKFAST TABLE.

From a close observation of Australian restaurants I have come to the conclusion that the Australian does not eat his food—he wolfs it. He's not very particular either what he eats. (In Queensland earth is in his dieting scale). What he chiefly wants is something to chew, and he usually bites off more than he comfortably can.

He's argumentative at the breakfast table, and the less he knows about a subject the more he'll say. One of him wanted to argue with me only the other morning on this very subject of eating. The argument turned on the word "dinner," and he let his porridge get cold while he went for a dictionary. "To dine," he said, with his mouth full, "is to 'take dinner,' and according to this dictionary that is 'the chief meal of the day.'" That's just it—the Australian regulates it by size; he cannot distinguish between a meal and a dinner.

Delicate glass, spotless napery, flowers, and above all sparkling conversation—those larger delights!—he does not encourage. He is a mere gross feeder. I am talking now of the man who can afford these things (even the employment of a conversationalist), not of the sixpenny "Dining" rooms, of which Australia is the home. How horrible these "dining" rooms are on a hot day! You can smell them two streets off. If you are brave enough to look in you will see what you usually go to the zoo at 4 o'clock to watch.

There is no restaurant in Australia where you can get a meal suited to the climate, and as for "home" meals, well, if an Australian asks you to his house to dine don't go unless you're an ostrich. Cooking among Australian women is a lost art. The Australian girl goes in for "accomplishments" only. If she is ever called upon to cook anything she uses the frypan.

If I ever set up business in Australia it would be in three "lines"—frying pans, false teeth, and patent medicines.

Everything is washed down in Australia with tea. It is a dangerous beverage as it is made there, in witness thereof are the clayey complexions and dyspeptic noses of the women. Why they don't drink wine, the natural beverage of the country, I never could make out until I tasted the vintages. But they are improving. Some foreigners are making very decent wine in Australia just now; but the Australians won't drink it until it is exported and returns again to the country with a French brand on it. The same remark applies to most things in Australia. They don't manufacture anything. I once dined with a squatter in Queensland, and there was not an article of furniture in the room that had been made in Australia, and not a thing on the table, except the vegetables, but was imported. The table linen, the glassware, the knives, the crockery—all were imported. The wine was imported, so was the salmon, and the coffee, and his "Missus's" cat was Manx. And yet there wasn't a thing in the room but the raw material could have been produced in the country, right down to the condiments.

CHAPTER XV.

THE AUSTRALIAN POETS.

When I went into the Public Library at Sydney and asked for the catalogue of the Australian poets I thought the attendant, in complying, had handed me the Federal electoral rolls. He said, however, that it was all right. There are just about as many people anxious to make the poetry of the country as there are to make its laws, and among them all they have made a mess of both. Parkes, addressing a public meeting, once said, "I would rather be a third-rate poet than a first-class politician." Somebody interjected: "Well, aren't you?" I thank God when I think of the few awful hours I spent with the Australian muse (or, more correctly speaking, bemuse) that I have read very little Australian poetry. Nevertheless I have read enough to enable me to arrive at a definition of what really constitutes a right to be called a poet, and it is: Any person of either sex who can write in metre without being laughed at. In applying this golden rule it will be seen that there are no poets in Australia except the alleged humorous versifiers.

Sir Henry Parkes, deceased, is generally referred to in the Australian Press as poet, politician and patriot. I haven't the time to inquire into all the other things, but I did spend an hour with his "Fragmentary Thoughts" and "Stolen Moments." They are well worth perusing, and I think everybody ought to read those sympathetic lines "To a Beautiful and Friendless Child; aged four years." The child was aged four years; it is not "an early poem," which fact I thought it just as well to mention before quoting the opening stanza:

"Did shock of birth-bliss slay thy mother?How from all kindred torn?Than God's all-seeing eye, what otherSaid that a man was born?"

But the poet is even better in his stirring moods, as in the well-known (in Australia) "Australian Youth's Song." Here is one of the "jewels four lines long":—

"We live in hope—we live in hope!Forget the day that's gone!Or dim or bright, the future's lightIs all to guide us on."

A strong man would shed tears over the same poet's "The Dying Convict's Letter." For that reason I shan't quote it any further than to say it begins:

"In mental agony he lifted upHis voice to Him who hears the sufferer's prayer...."

That's just what you feel like doing. The spirit of humility expressed in the poem is in sharp contrast to the ferocity expressed by a brother bard, who, on leaving Australia's shores, shook his clenched fist at the continent and recited some lines ending—

"The rich man's Heaven, the poor man's Hell,Land of — —, Fare thee well!"

There has been a lot of controversy in the Commonwealth as to the missing word, so I leave it blank, and pass on to the ode that won the New South Wales Government prize of fifty guineas, in open competition, as being the best "Occasional" for the birth of the Commonwealth. Listen to the opening:

"Awake! Arise! The wings of dawnAre beating at the Gates of Day!"

And that was addressed to the Australian for the purpose of arousing him! What chance had it of doing so; the Australian merely turned over and said, "Why the blanky blank should I get up?" It's just as well that all should know here and now that the only way to waken Australia is to heave a brick at it—same as I'm doing.

One of the best known poets of Australia, I understand, is the Rev. Mr. Cuzens, who published a volume entitled "Footprints of Jesus." I make bold to reprint a verse of "The Temptation":

"A dreary wilderness, a desert wildOf Nature's varied loveliness despoiled,Stretched out, I see, in barrenness and woeA fitting emblem of the world below;Deep gloom and dreadThe land o'erspread."

I cannot say of what denomination the rev. poet was; but I understand it was written before the days of the Salvation Army commenced to enrich the world's library of hymns.

There was also a poet named Kendall, of whom Australia is very proud. The Press critics call him an "impulsive songster," and I do remember taking a little thing of his away in memory after reading a collection of his verse. The little thing went:

"There is a river in the hillsI long to think about,Perhaps the searching feet of manHave never found it out."

It suggested to me at the time "Mary had a little lamb"—slightly uneven in the feet. Kendall was accused of purloining from Tennyson, and he explained—"We cannot pass through the woods without taking away the smell of violets." But that wasn't the charge; it was that he dug the violets up by the roots and transplanted them in his own pages. But Kendall has gone; he has also his reward. I saw a life-sized painting of him in the hall of a Sydney sporting hotel when I was staying there. For what more can a poet ask in Australia?

Brunton Stephens, though he wrote in Australia, received his impression and education in the old world. He did not adopt Australia till he was 31 years of age, and a man gathers few new impressions after thirty; he lives in and writes of those of youth. Thus, strictly speaking, Stephens was not an Australian poet. Yet he was the only man in the country who ever wrote with a philosophic outlook (and a knowledge of prosody). He was not an admirer of Australian poetry either: "It lacks a fundamental basis of brain" was his verdict. Poor Stephens, Stephens the stickler for the precise word, the admirer of literary craftsmanship—this is what he got at the hands of an Australian bard, who wrote a critical biography of him on the literary page of the National newspaper; mine are the italics and parenthetical remarks:

"He was the youngest of a family of six—two brothers and three sisters." (Stephens once taught mathematics.)

"Fielding, Smollett, Shakespeare, and the English classics were more to the boy's taste than athletics...." (What nationality were F., S. and S.?)

"At 11 his father died...."(!)

"The position was secured for him through the influence of a fellow student named Simpson, whose father later on became the discoverer of chloroform as an anaesthetic—and a knight." (Intrepid Simpson's father.)

"They (the Leylands) literally rolled in riches."

"Within a week he delivered a lecture on 'The Antiquities of Egypt' in the Brisbane School of Arts." (! again).

"Men of Stephens' temperament too often have made mistakes in marrying—it is sufficient to say that Stephens married the predestined woman." (As a matter of fact Stephens was most happily married.)

I merely mention these things to show how they treat a poet in Australia.

For the rest, the Australian poets are pessimists, alleged funny writers, and parodists of Swinburne and Kipling. Paterson's writings smell of horse sweat and stable sweepings. Lawson sings of Colonial beer—which, dear English reader, God spare you from ever tasting—Daley retails the philosophy of that blasphemous old reprobate, Omar, with this difference—a pewter of Colonial beer, not a jug of wine. And then there are Gordon, and Sladen, John Cash Neild, Mr. Furtell and Farrell. The last mentioned wrote a poem "How he Died." I've never read it, and don't want to, so can't say how he died. But if it was an Australian poet who was dying I know how he ought to have been killed. In the pleasant metaphor of his own country, he should have got it where the chicken got the axe.

CHAPTER XVI.

THE C.Y.A.

This title, which attaches to all Australians during a period of superficial precocity, has great local significance. It means clever young Australian, and it originated in the newspapers, where the phrases are the same yesterday, to-day, and for ever. For instance, no Australian editor would let the name of Chatterton pass without adding "Wonderful boy."

C.Y.A. is, therefore, a newspaper degree. It is conferred most heartily—and with rather less discrimination than Ally Sloper's award of merit—by junior reporters. Mothers just yearn for it, and the local newspaper is obliging.

An Australian mother tells her daughters to be clever—and let who will be good. The result is much cultivated mediocrity—mechanical pianists, and thin voices taught to sing Tosti's "Goodbye" for the inevitable subscription concert to raise funds for further futile study. There is in every town in the Commonwealth, a coming Australian, but none of them ever seem to do any arriving. Someone is, all the same, for ever getting a benefit (of the doubt) in the shape of the aforesaid subscription concert. It is given out that she is going to the old world to study under Marchesi or someone sufficiently afar to make the passage money a consideration. It's a regular confidence trick, for no sooner does the shock of the beneficiary's awful singing blow over, than she is back about town again. Perhaps she has realised enough by the fraud to buy a piano and a brass plate and she sets up teaching others to follow in her devious ways.

Strict justice to the Australian songster compels me to say that a few of them do achieve to the position of chorus girls. I heard some chorus girls of the old school complain in a café one night that "what with these Conservatorium girls cutting the screws the profession is going to the dogs."

There have been some Australian women who have reached London and hit that city hard. Melba—Nellie Armstrong that was—managed it. She was not a C.Y.A., however. She has outlived one of the adjectives before she went "Home." When she was singing at shilling concerts her fellow Australians hadn't the gumption to hear anything wonderful in her notes. Melba recently swept through Australia in a semi-regal way, and was queen of a champion grovelling match.

Ada Crossley also found London. She came back and found Australia, which wouldn't look at her at a 1/- some years before when her notes were fuller and richer, ready to pay half a guinea a time of its creditors' money to see what her gowns were like.

Of the many other singers who left Australia's shores the most have been engulfed in the city of the Thames. Some bob up now and again, when their voices are to be heard at pops. But most of them would like to raise a return fare, and that is probably their last illusion.

And then, of course, the stage attracts the C.Y.A. Anything that looks easy and is likely to bring adulation always does. But I have made exhaustive inquiry and failed to discover one actor or actress who learnt the business in Australia that has turned out anything worth mentioning. I have traced several to London and there given them up—the men in pity and the women in disgust.

The founder of the drama in Australia was Barrington, a convict-actor. Some idea of his ability as an actor may be formed from the fact that he was ever convicted.

In the drama Oscar Asche is the only man I can find doing fairly well, but he did not learn his business in Australia. Indeed, it is part of Australia's ignominy to see English and American artists being imported to play any parts requiring the exercise of intelligence. Managers, when interviewed as to why they don't employ Australians have given it as a reason that the Australians cannot pronounce English properly, and that they have a distorted idea of love-making. The fact is that by the time the Australian gets a part he is so furtive with dodging creditors that he cannot get apprehension out of his face when any other character makes an entrance.

The artistic Australian also gets to London. Mortimer Menpes was a C.Y.A. He went from Adelaide—a town which also produced the late Mr. Guy

Boothby, C.Y.A. Menpes, in writing his biography for "Who's Who," stated that he was "inartistically born in Australia." What does he mean? He was before the time of incubators.

Then Boothby—late Guy Boothby! I don't know how he could ever have looked a bookstall in the face after what he wrote—or his fellow Australians. Nat Gould or Fergus Hume either, for that matter. Between them these Australians used to average four books a month, fifteen short stories and two puff interviews by Mr. Boothby with himself, written up for the magazines. Mr. Boothby found plenty of good material in himself for interviews. Haddon Chambers, C.Y.A., also gives the magazine readers glimpses of himself, but of late years he seems to spend all his time in protesting that he did write the "Tyranny of Tears."

Then in the realm of high art is Longstaff, C.Y.A., painter, Mackennal, C.Y.A., sculptor. The first is head and shoulders above the other Australian daubers, but he'd have to get on stilts and wear the highest stove pipe to be classed eminent in London; the second gets odd jobs which the cableman chronicles betimes.

Probably if you asked any Australian the best Australian book he would say "For the Term of His Natural Life," by Marcus Clark. Well, I just recently read in Duffy's "Life of Two Hemispheres," that Charles Gavan Duffy wrote it. He particularly says so.

Rolfe Boldrewood, C.Y.A., is also classed a literary man in Australia. He wrote numerous tales of colonial improbabilities.

There is a paper in London called the "British Australasian," and it follows the doings of the C.Y.A.'s in London as far as it can with self-respect. But when frequent changes of address make it too plain that the C.Y.A. is bilking his landlady, and the change of locality is from humble to worse—well, it discreetly draws the curtain. The "British Australasian" is a most genteel publication. It was one of the first to drop De Rougemont, C.Y.A.